Night and Day

Written by Marilyn Minkoff
Illustrated by Michael Grejniec

Modern Curriculum Press
A Division of Simon & Schuster
299 Jefferson Road, P.O. Box 480
Parsippany, NJ 07054 - 0480

Design and production by Kirchoff/Wohlberg, Inc.

ISBN: 0-8136-0813-9 Modern Curriculum Press

3 4 5 6 7 8 9 10 SP 01 00 99 98 97

Once long ago,

the sun was everywhere.

"I need to sleep," said the sun.

"Stay up," said the flowers.
"We grow in the sun."

"Stay up," said the animals.
"We run in the sun."

"Stay up," said the children.
"We have fun in the sun."

"I need to take a nap," said the sun.

And that is what the sun did.

"Where is the sun?" said the flowers.
"We can't grow."

"Where is the sun?" said the animals.
"We can't run."

"Where is the sun?" said the children.
"We can't have fun."

"Get up, sun," they said.
"Get up!"

"I must sleep now," said the sun.
"Go away."

"I'll be back tomorrow."